PATTERN PROJECTS

BUGS

by Marilynn G. Barr

Publisher: Roberta Suid

Production: Little Acorn & Associates, Inc.

MM2194
PATTERN PROJECTS: BUGS

Entire contents copyright © 2005
by Monday Morning Books, Inc.

For a complete Catalog, write to the address below:
Monday Morning Books, Inc.
PO Box 1134
Inverness, CA 94937

Call our toll-free number: 1-800-255-6049
E-mail us at: MMBooks@aol.com
Visit our Web site:
http://www.mondaymorningbooks.com

Monday Morning is a registered trademark of
Monday Morning Books, Inc.
For more products featuring art by Marilynn G. Barr visit www.littleacornbooks.com

ISBN 1-57612-221-2

Printed in the United States of America
9 8 7 6 5 4 3 2 1

Contents

Introduction

Reinforce skills practice with the activities and patterns in *Pattern Projects: Bugs*. Children find bugs fascinating and will enjoy making bug costumes and props using construction paper, brown grocery bags, and craft sticks. Provide ladybug, spots, bees, and hive patterns for children to practice alphabet or counting skills. Make a "Flower Trail" game board for children to practice counting skills. Decorate display boards and work folders with dragonflies, bees, ladybugs, and other insect patterns and borders. Reproduce bookmarks for children to use while developing their reading skills. Bug cards (pp. 49-58) are designed with gray tone bug illustrations to allow for readability when programmed. Bug card illustrations can be traced over with a black marker for alternate uses.

Bug Costumes and Props

Wand Masks

Materials: construction paper, mask patterns, crayons, markers, scissors, glue, large craft sticks

Reproduce a bug mask pattern for each child. Provide crayons or markers and scissors for children to color and cut out masks. Then help each child glue a large craft stick to the back of the mask to form a wand mask.

Headbands

Materials: poster board, headband patterns, crayons, markers, scissors, glue, tape

Cut a poster board or oak tag headband for each child. Provide children with insect headband patterns to color and cut out. Help each child glue the patterns onto a headband. Then wrap and tape each child's headband to fit.

MM2194 • Pattern Projects: Bugs • ©2005 Monday Morning Books, Inc.

Bug Costumes and Props

Brown Grocery Bag Vests

Materials: brown grocery bags, bug costume patterns, crayons, markers, scissors, glue, yarn, stapler

Each child will need a brown grocery bag to make a vest to match his or her bug mask and headband. Help each child cut a brown grocery bag to form a vest as shown on each costume patterns page. Have children color, cut out, and glue patterns onto their grocery bag vests. Then cut and staple yarn ties to each child's vest.

Wand Puppets

Materials: construction paper, bug puppet patterns, crayons, markers, scissors, glue, craft sticks

Reproduce construction paper puppet patterns for children to make wand puppets to use during a story hour. Have children color and cut out puppet patterns. Then help each child glue a craft stick to the back of his or her puppet.

Cereal Box Totes

Materials: cereal boxes, construction paper, farm animal patterns, crayons, markers, scissors, hole punch, yarn

Cut off the tops of the cereal boxes. Help children cover boxes with colored construction paper. Then have children color and cut out bug patterns to decorate the boxes. Children glue their cutouts to the boxes. Punch two holes along each long side to thread and tie yarn handles as shown here. Other dry food boxes can be used to make different-sized totes.

Pocket Puppets

Materials: paper plates, bug mask patterns, crayons, markers, scissors, stapler

Nest and cut away 1/4 of two paper plates for each child. With insides facing each other, staple the plates together to form a pocket. Provide bug mask patterns for children to color, cut out, and glue to paper plate pockets.

Bug Games

Bug Bingo

Materials: oak tag, bingo board and card patterns, crayons, markers, scissors, manila envelope for storage

Reproduce, color, cut out, and laminate oak tag bingo boards and tokens. Reproduce, color, laminate, then cut apart a set of bingo cards. To play: Provide each child with a bingo card and tokens. Shuffle, then draw a card from the top of the deck. Call out the name of the bug as you show the card to the players. Instruct children to place a token on the matching square. The first child with three tokens in a row (horizontally, vertically, or diagonally) wins.

Bug Match

Materials: oak tag, match board and card patterns, crayons, markers, scissors, manila envelope

Reproduce, color, cut out, and laminate oak tag bug match boards. Reproduce, color, laminate, and cut apart two sets of bug cards. Decorate a manila envelope and use to store match boards and cards. For two players: Each player takes a match board. One player shuffles and places the cards, face down, on the playing surface. Each player, in turn, draws a card. If the card matches, the player places the card on the matching square on his or her match board. If the player already has made the match, the player returns the card to the bottom of the deck. The first player to fill his or her board, wins.

Bug Games

Flower Trail Game Board

Materials: oak tag, construction paper, crayons, markers, scissors, glue, brad, pawns

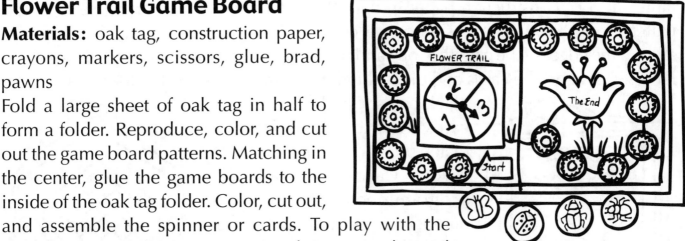

Fold a large sheet of oak tag in half to form a folder. Reproduce, color, and cut out the game board patterns. Matching in the center, glue the game boards to the inside of the oak tag folder. Color, cut out, and assemble the spinner or cards. To play with the spinner: Each player, in turn, spins then moves his or her pawn the number of spaces indicated on the spinner. To play with cards: Reproduce and place two sets of cards face down on the game board. Each player draws a card and moves to the matching space. The first player to reach The End, wins.

Bug Tank Bulletin Board

Cover your display board with green bulletin board paper. Cut two black poster board strips for the top and bottom of the bug tank. Have children color and cut out bug patterns. Cut brown construction paper twigs and green construction paper leaves. Assemble the twigs, leaves, and cutout bugs on the board. Measure, cut, and attach a sheet of cellophane over the twigs, leaves, and bugs. Then attach the black poster board strips to the top and bottom of your Bug Tank.

Bug Skills Practice

Prepare shape work folders for children to practice alphabet or number skills. Fold a large sheet of construction paper in half. Reproduce, color, cut, and glue a garden pattern (pp. 59-69) to one side of the construction paper folder. Staple, then trim around the edges of the pattern. Copy and program bug cards with upper and lowercase letters. Cut apart the cards and place them inside the shape work folder. Discard the

blank cards. Children remove all cards from the shape folder to match upper and lowercase letter cards. Cards can also be programmed with numerals, number words, and number sets (1-10) for number skills practice.

Bug Folder Toppers

Materials: manila folders, construction paper, bug folder toppers, crayons, markers, scissors, glue

Provide children with bug folder topper patterns to color and cut out. Help each child glue the folder topper patterns onto manila file folders. Folders can be used to store children's unfinished work or for finished work display during open house.

Bug Button Bookmarks

Materials: oak tag, bug button bookmark patterns, crayons, markers

Reproduce and cut apart oak tag bug button bookmark patterns. Provide crayons and markers for children to color the bookmarks.

Bug Borders

Materials: oak tag, bug borders, construction paper, crayons, markers, scissors

Reproduce, color, and cut out bug borders. Use bug borders to decorate bulletin boards, folders, and desks. Borders can also be used to make headbands and decorate storage containers.

Bug Patterns
Butterfly

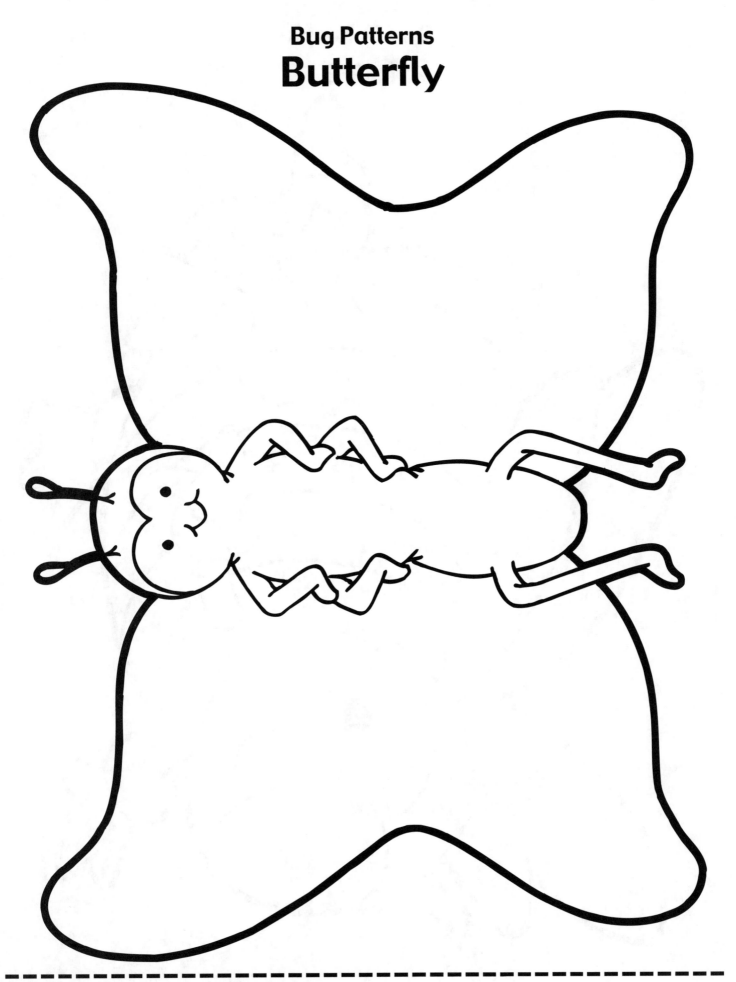

 MM2194 • Pattern Projects: Bugs • ©2005 Monday Morning Books, Inc.

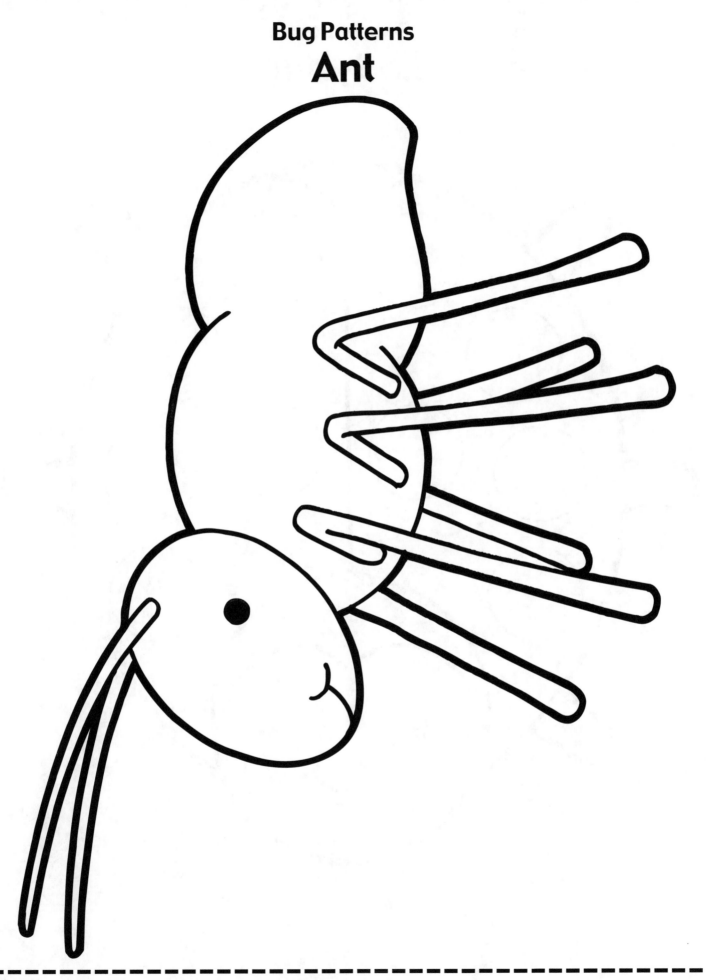

MM2194 • Pattern Projects: Bugs • ©2005 Monday Morning Books, Inc.

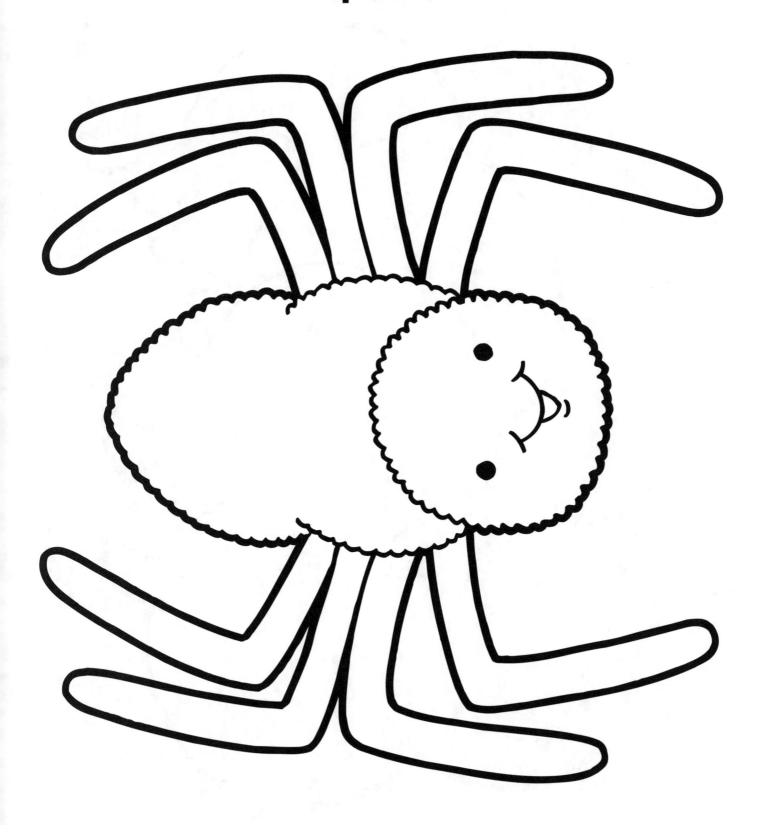

Beetle

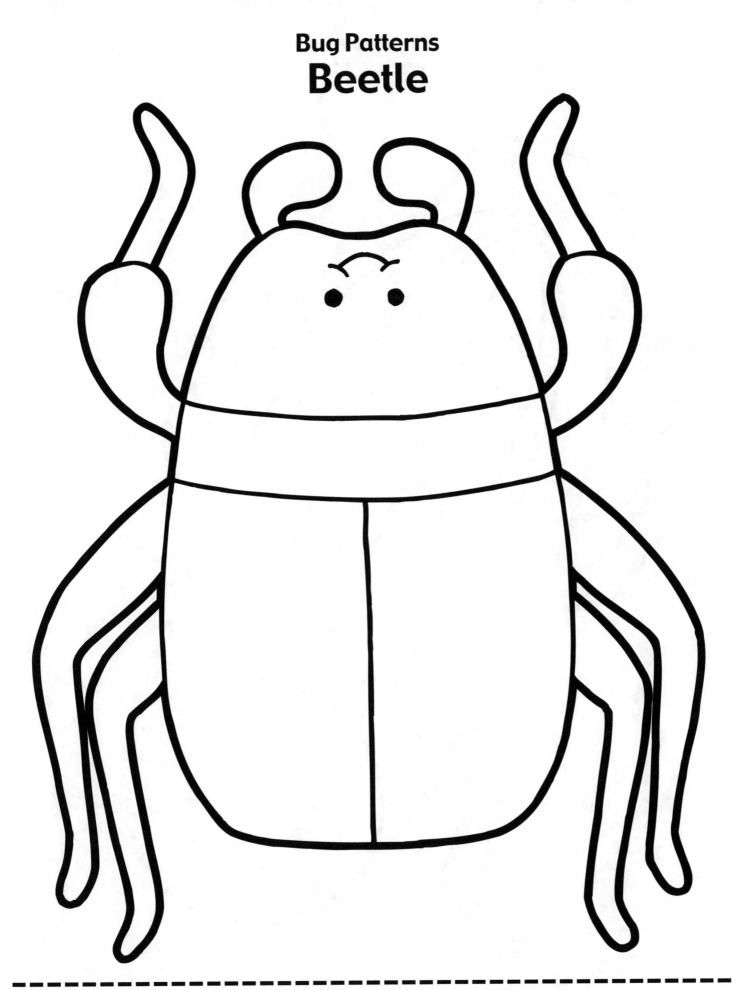

Firefly

MM2194 • Pattern Projects: Bugs • ©2005 Monday Morning Books, Inc.

Grasshopper

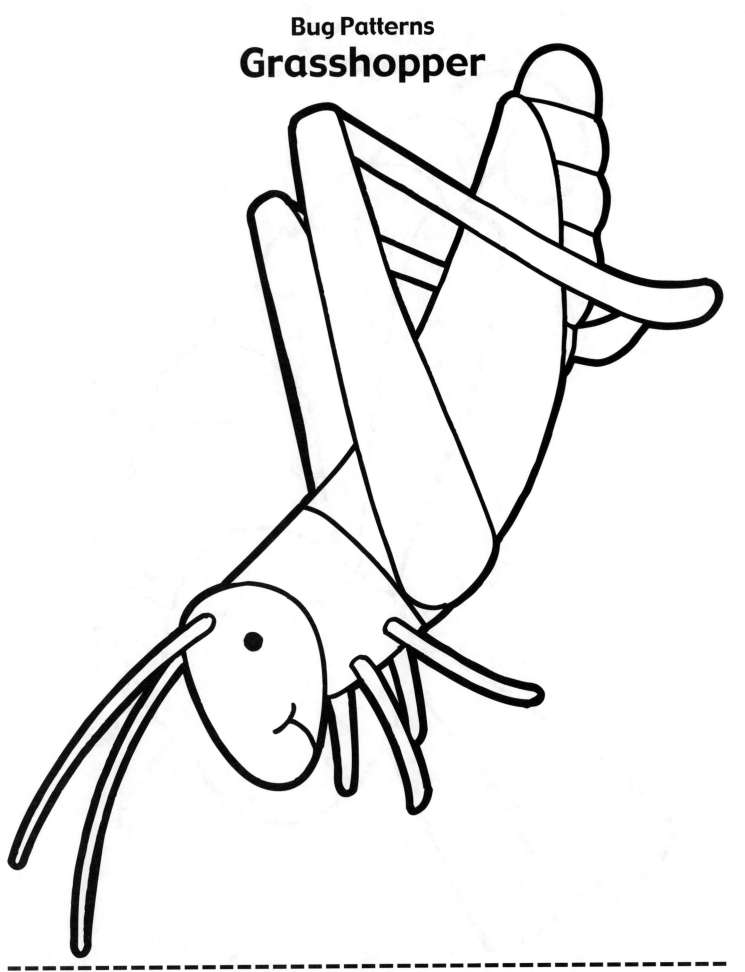

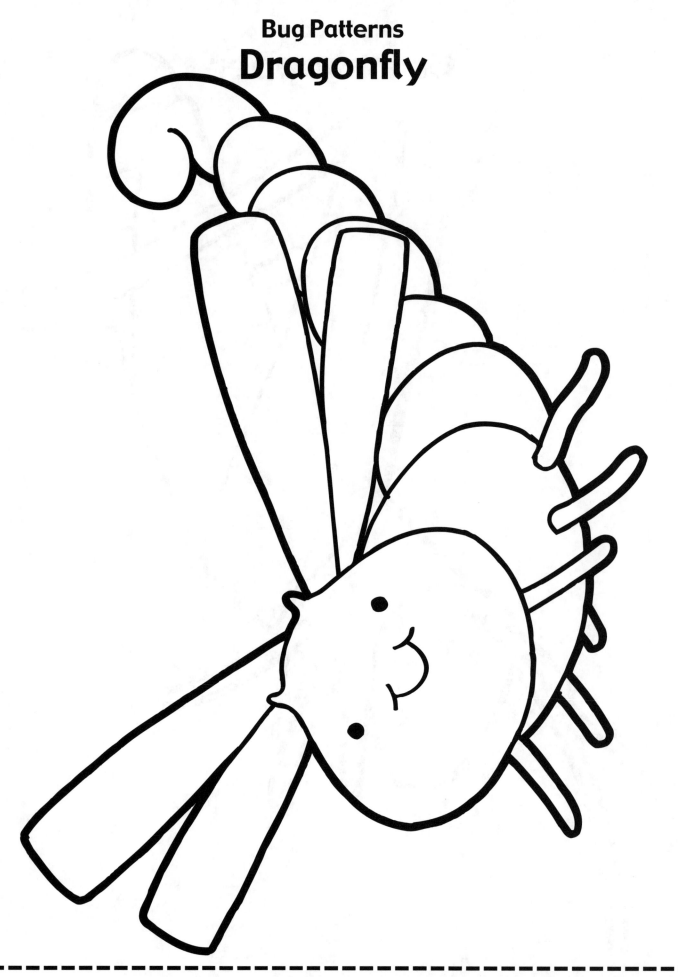

MM2194 • Pattern Projects: Bugs • ©2005 Monday Morning Books, Inc.

Bug Costume Patterns
Butterfly Mask

Cut and glue pipe cleaner antennae to the butterfly mask.

Bug Costume Patterns
Butterfly Wing

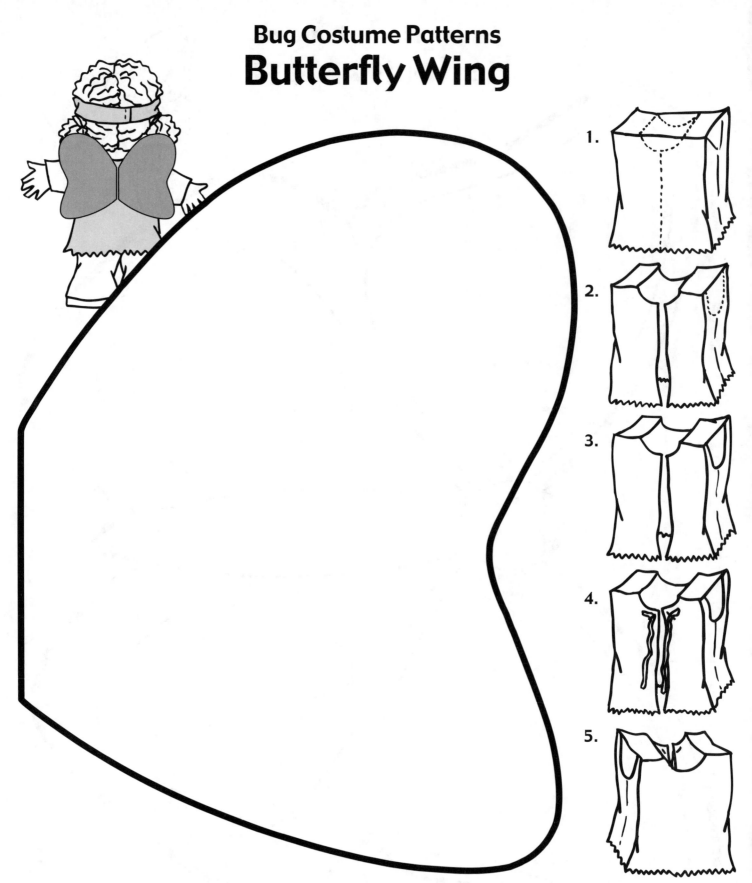

Butterfly grocery bag vests can only be worn with the opening in front.

Color, cut out, and glue two construction paper wings to the grocery bag costume vest.

Option: Make matching-colored construction paper headbands.

MM2194 • Pattern Projects: Bugs • ©2005 Monday Morning Books, Inc.

Bee Mask

Color, cut out, and glue the antennae to the bee mask as shown here.

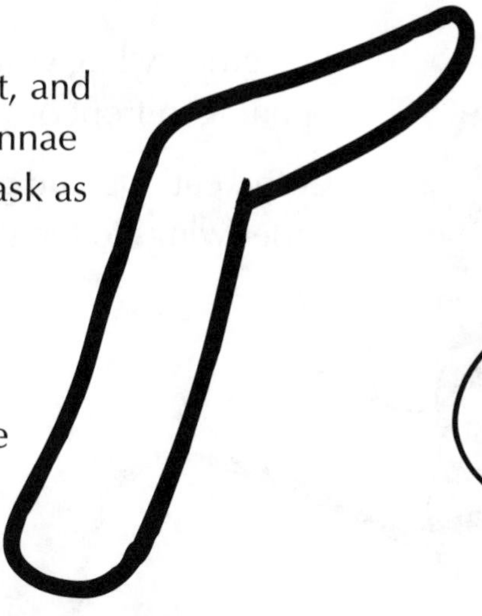

Antennae

Bug Costume Patterns
Bee Wings

Bee grocery bag vests can be worn with the opening in front or back.

Color, cut out, and glue two sets of construction paper wings to the grocery bag costume vest.

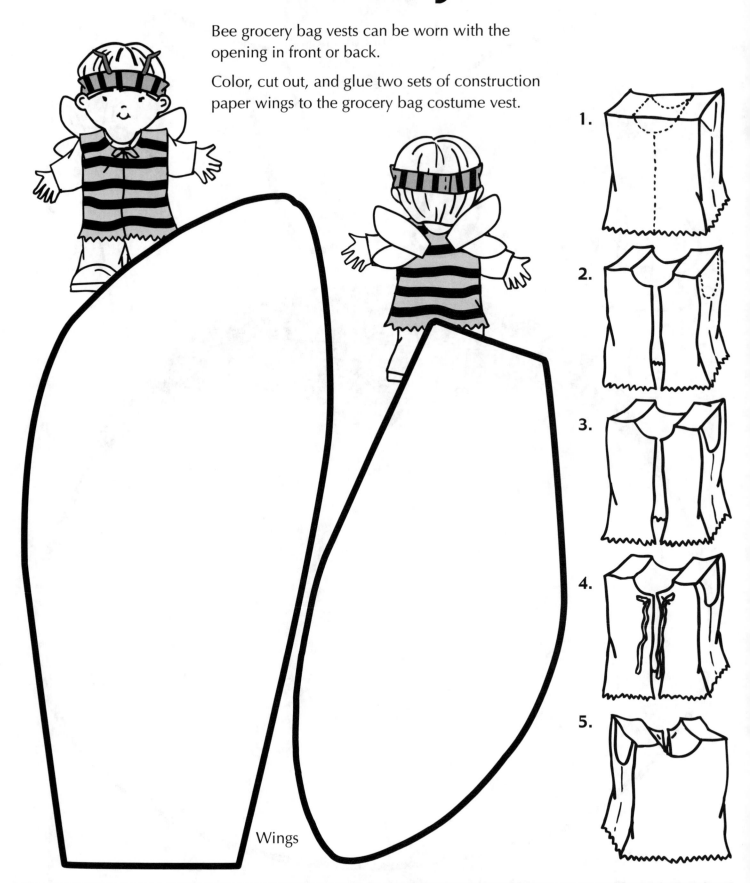

1.

2.

3.

4.

5.

Wings

MM2194 • Pattern Projects: Bugs • ©2005 Monday Morning Books, Inc.

Bug Costume Patterns
Ant Mask

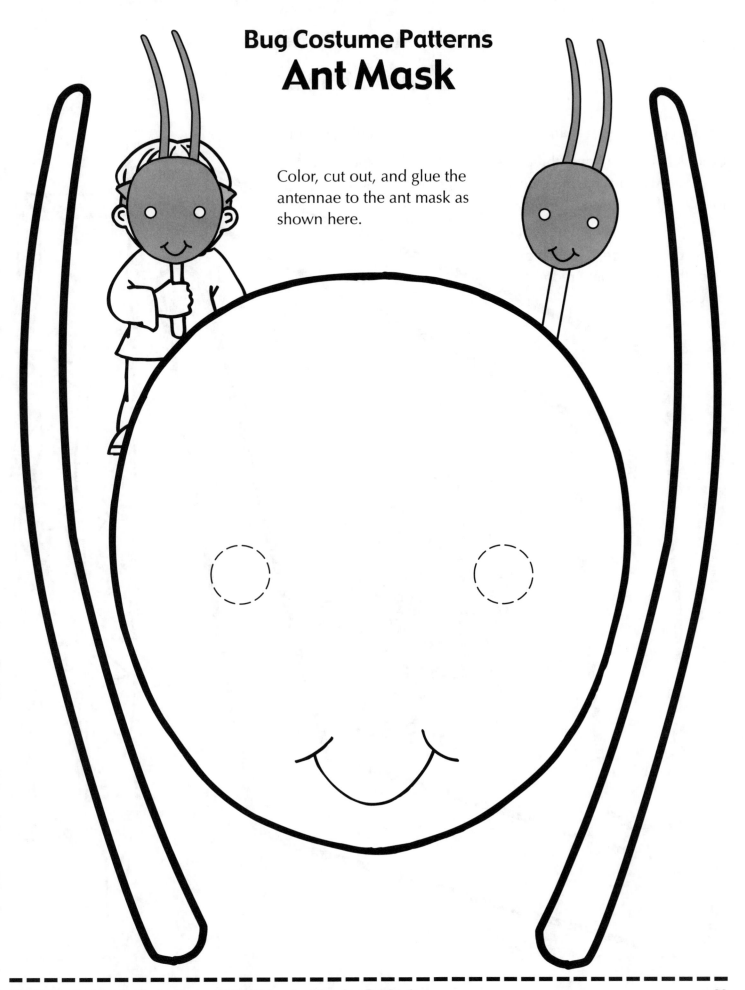

Color, cut out, and glue the antennae to the ant mask as shown here.

Bug Costume Patterns
Ant Legs

Ant grocery bag vests can only be worn with the opening in front.

Color, cut out, and glue three sets of construction paper legs to the vest. Also cut out and glue a circle and oval to the vest to form an ant body.

Option: Make matching-colored construction paper headbands. Paint the ant costume red, black, or brown.

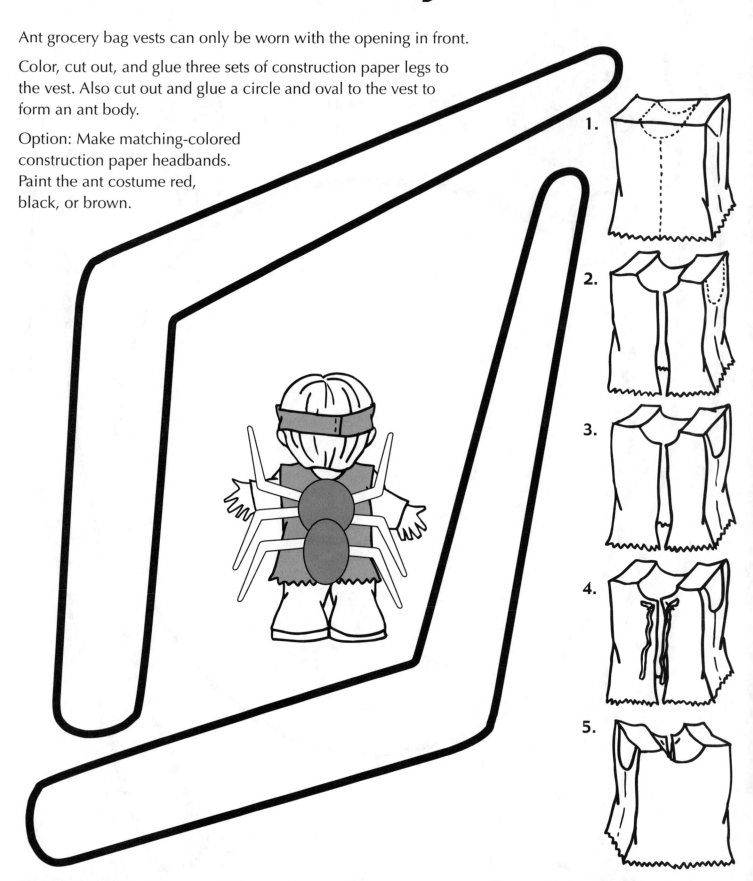

1.

2.

3.

4.

5.

MM2194 • Pattern Projects: Bugs • ©2005 Monday Morning Books, Inc.

Bug Costume Patterns
Ladybug Mask

Cut out and color a construction paper circle to resemble a ladybug shell. Glue the circle to the ladybug mask as shown here.

Ladybug Wings

1.

2.

3.

4.

5.

Ladybug grocery bag vests can only be worn with the opening in front.

Color, cut out, and glue two construction paper wings to the grocery bag costume vest.

Option: Make matching-colored construction paper headbands.

MM2194 • Pattern Projects: Bugs • ©2005 Monday Morning Books, Inc.

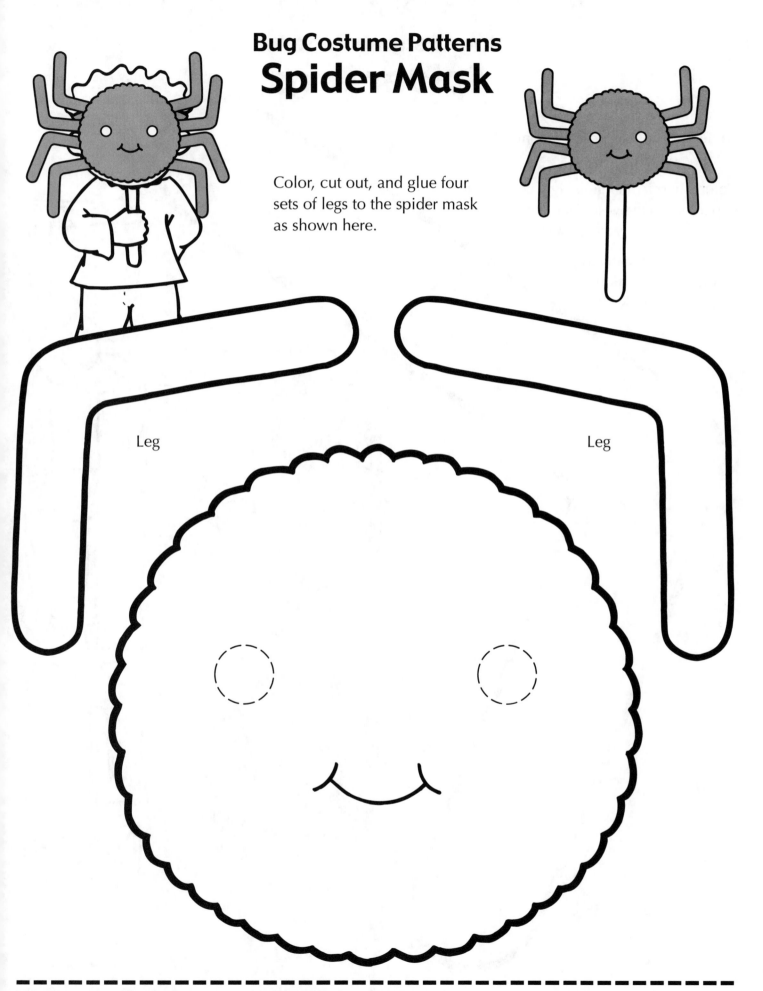

Bug Costume Patterns
Spider Mask

Color, cut out, and glue four sets of legs to the spider mask as shown here.

Leg

Leg

Bug Costume Patterns
Spider Legs

Spider grocery bag vests can only be worn with the opening in front.

Color, cut out, and glue eight construction paper legs to the vest. Then cut out and glue a circle body to the vest.

Option: Make matching-colored construction paper headbands.

1.

2.

3.

4.

5.

MM2194 • PATTERN PROJECTS: Bugs • ©2005 Monday Morning Books, Inc.

Bug Costume Patterns
Caterpillar Mask

Color, cut out, and glue construction paper body segments to the caterpillar mask as shown here.

Caterpillar Body Segments

Caterpillar grocery bag vests can only be worn with the opening in front.

Color, cut out, and glue four or more construction paper body segments to the grocery bag costume vest.

Option: Cut out segments from different colors or material (corrugated board, fun fur). Make matching-colored construction paper headbands.

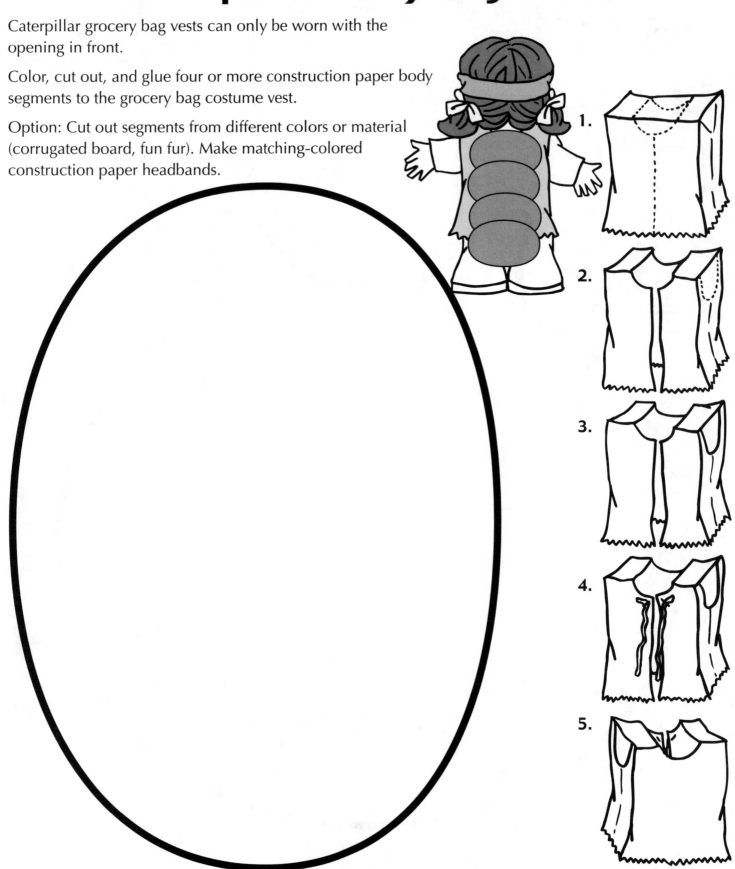

1.

2.

3.

4.

5.

Bug Costume Patterns
Beetle Mask

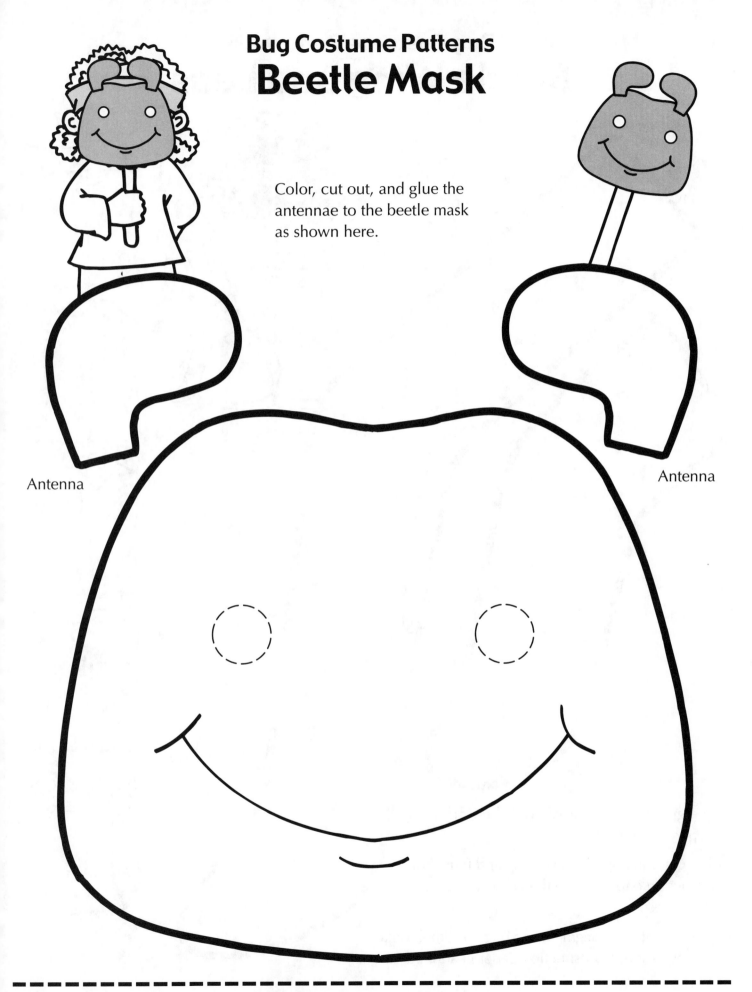

Color, cut out, and glue the antennae to the beetle mask as shown here.

Antenna

Antenna

Beetle Wing and Legs

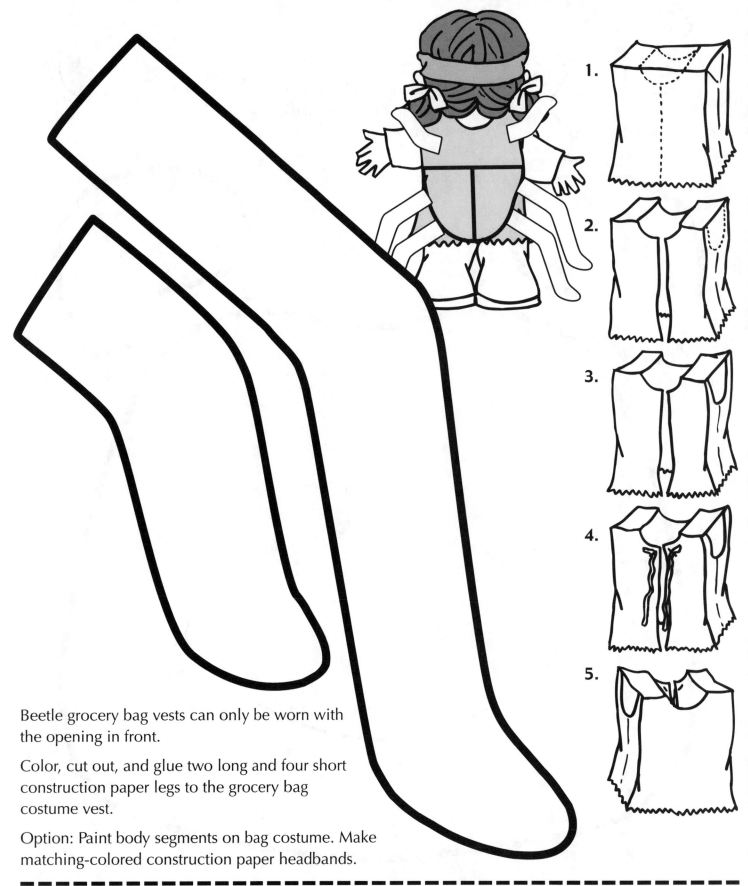

1.

2.

3.

4.

5.

Beetle grocery bag vests can only be worn with the opening in front.

Color, cut out, and glue two long and four short construction paper legs to the grocery bag costume vest.

Option: Paint body segments on bag costume. Make matching-colored construction paper headbands.

Firefly Mask

Color, cut out, and glue two construction paper wings (p. 34) and light to the firefly mask as shown here.

Light

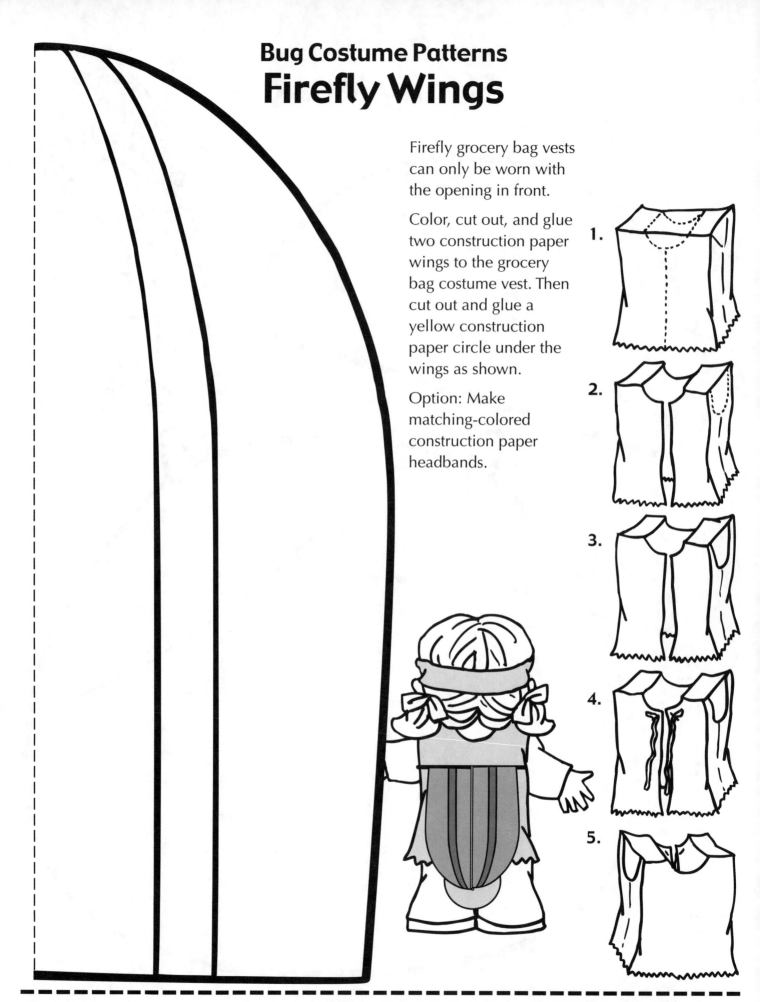

Bug Costume Patterns
Firefly Wings

Firefly grocery bag vests can only be worn with the opening in front.

Color, cut out, and glue two construction paper wings to the grocery bag costume vest. Then cut out and glue a yellow construction paper circle under the wings as shown.

Option: Make matching-colored construction paper headbands.

1.

2.

3.

4.

5.

MM2194 • Pattern Projects: Bugs • ©2005 Monday Morning Books, Inc.

Bug Costume Patterns
Grasshopper Mask

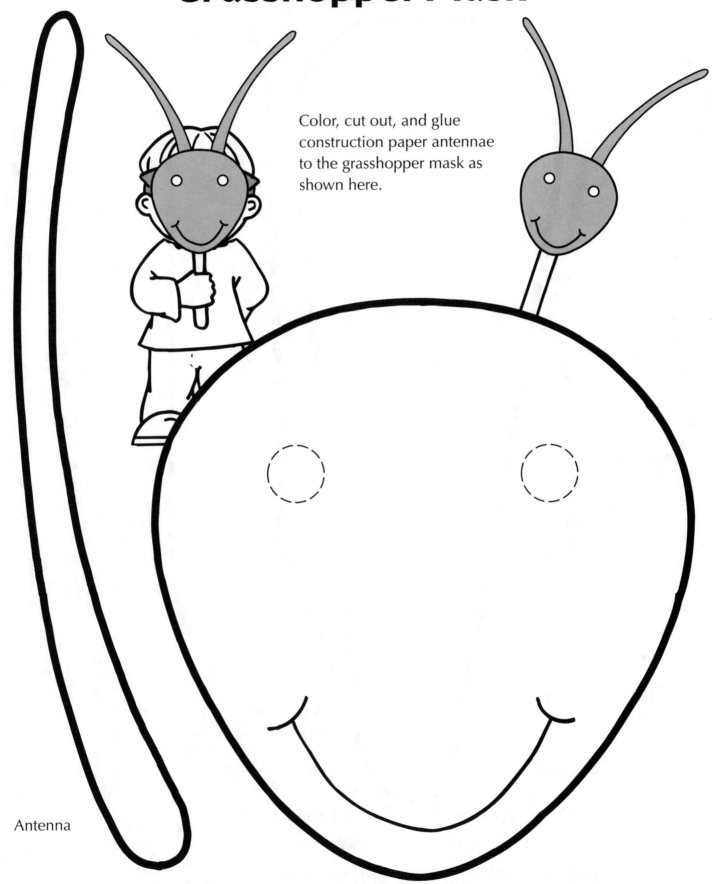

Color, cut out, and glue construction paper antennae to the grasshopper mask as shown here.

Antenna

Bug Costume Patterns
Grasshopper Legs

Short Leg
Cut four short legs.

Hinged Leg

Y

Y

Cut two sets of hinged legs. Glue the "Y" ends together, Then glue each hinged leg to the bag costume.

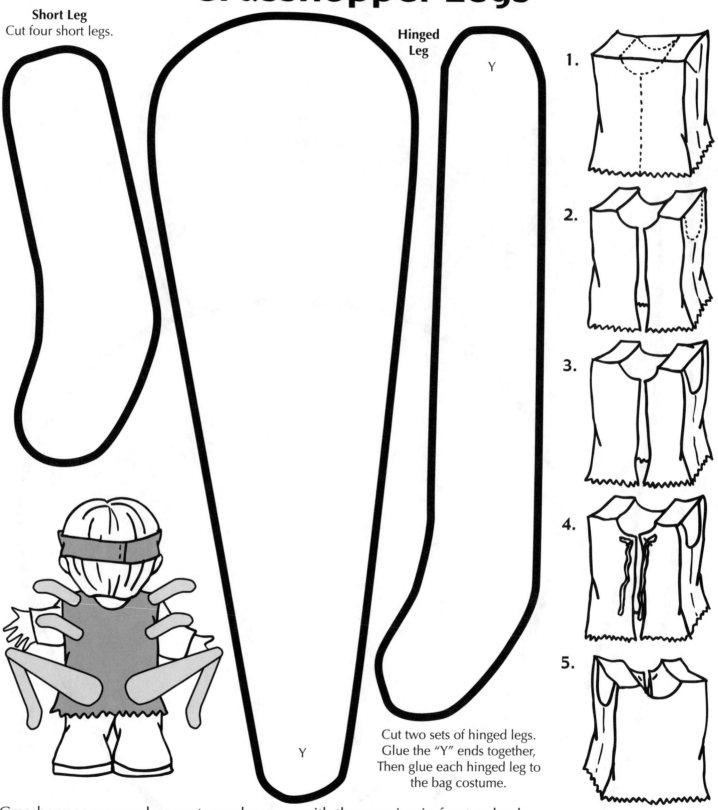

1.

2.

3.

4.

5.

Grasshopper grocery bag vests can be worn with the opening in front or back.

Color, cut out, and glue oak tag legs to the grocery bag costume vest.

Option: Make matching-colored construction paper headbands.

MM2194 • Pattern Projects: Bugs • ©2005 Monday Morning Books, Inc.

Color, cut out, and glue four construction paper wings to the dragonfly mask as shown here.

Bug Costume Patterns
Dragonfly Mask

Wing

Bug Costume Patterns
Dragonfly Wing

Dragonfly grocery bag vests can be worn with the opening in front or back.

Color, cut out, and glue four construction paper wings to the grocery bag costume vest.

Option: Paint the wings bright colors. Make matching-colored construction paper headbands.

1.

2.

3.

4.

5.

MM2194 • Pattern Projects: Bugs • ©2005 Monday Morning Books, Inc.

Butterflies

Bug Puppets
Ants

 MM2194 • Pattern Projects: Bugs • ©2005 Monday Morning Books, Inc.

Bug Puppets
Bees

 MM2194 • Pattern Projects: Bugs • ©2005 Monday Morning Books, Inc.

Caterpillars

MM2194 • Pattern Projects: Bugs • ©2005 Monday Morning Books, Inc.

Bug Puppets
Beetles

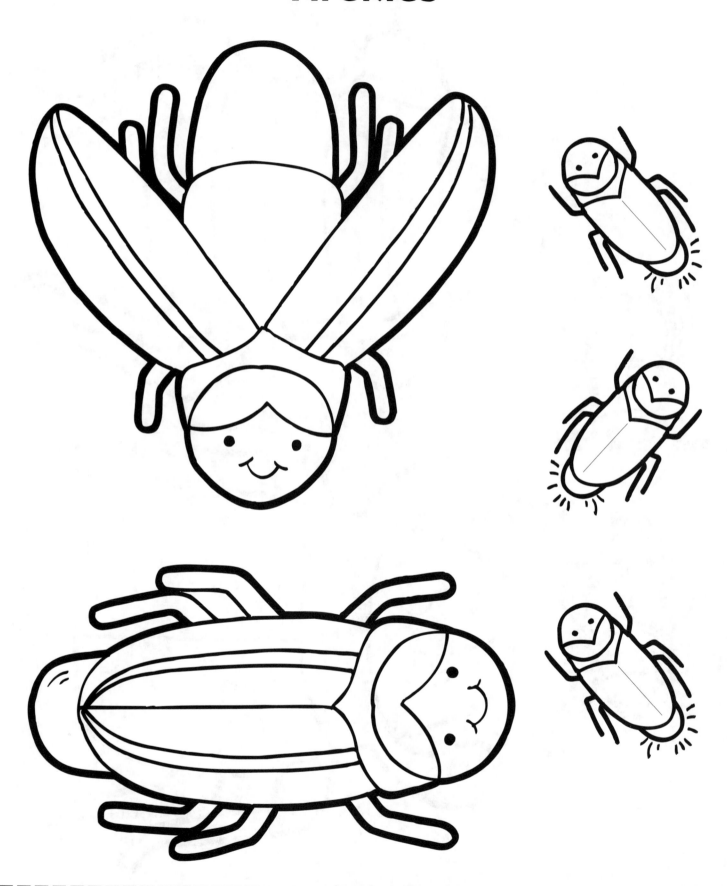

Grasshoppers

Butterflies

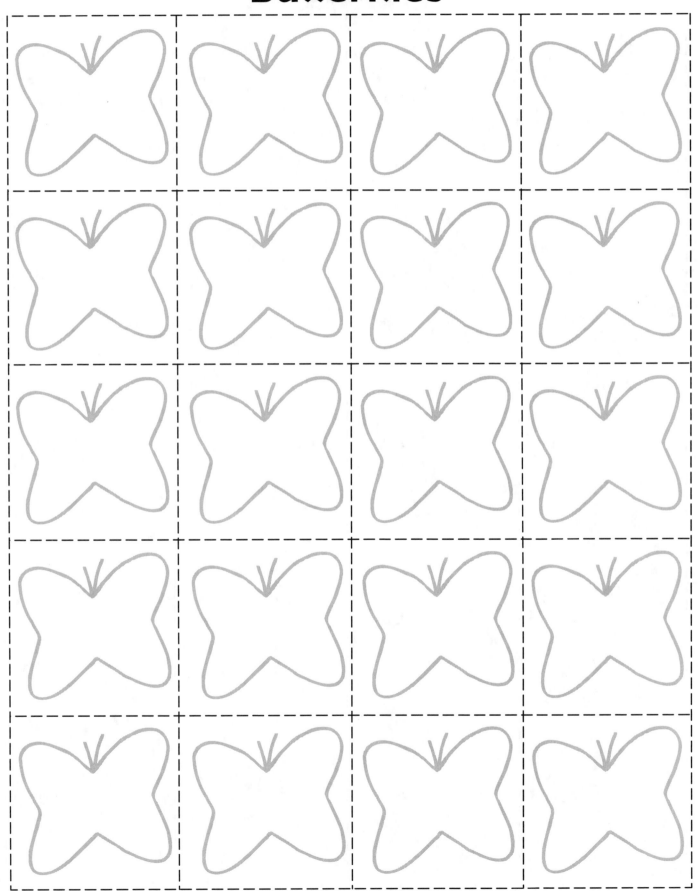

Bees

MM2194 • Pattern Projects: Bugs • ©2005 Monday Morning Books, Inc.

Bug Cards
Ants

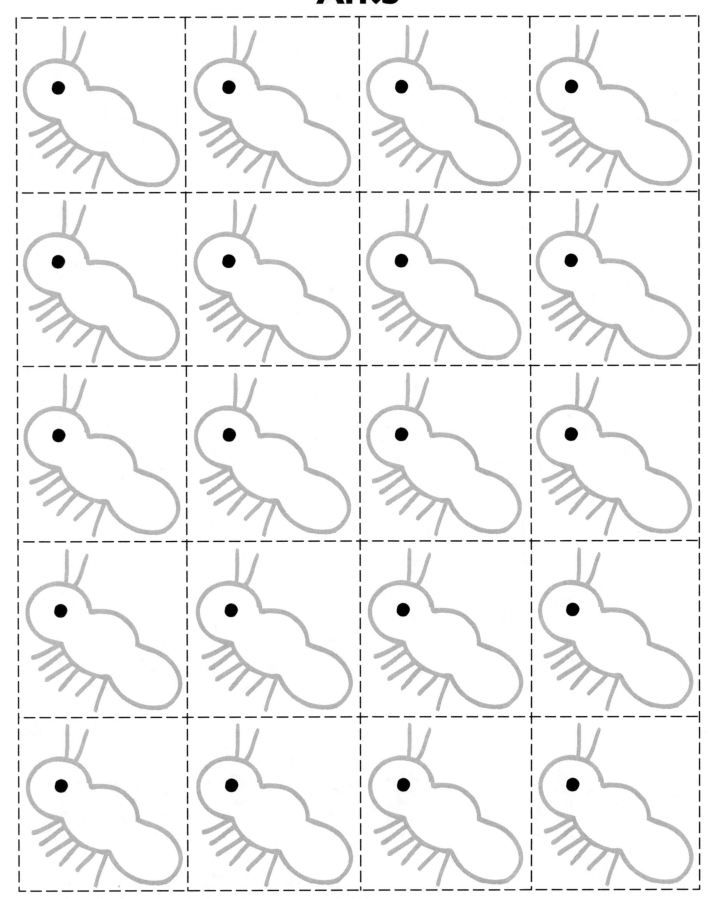

Bug Cards
Ladybugs

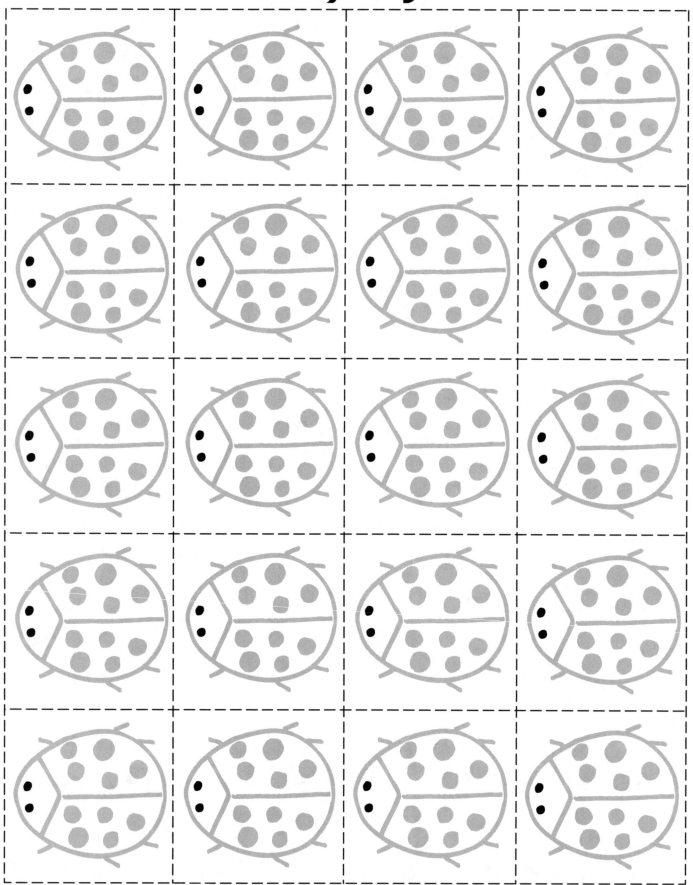

 MM2194 • Pattern Projects: Bugs • ©2005 Monday Morning Books, Inc.

Bug Cards
Spiders

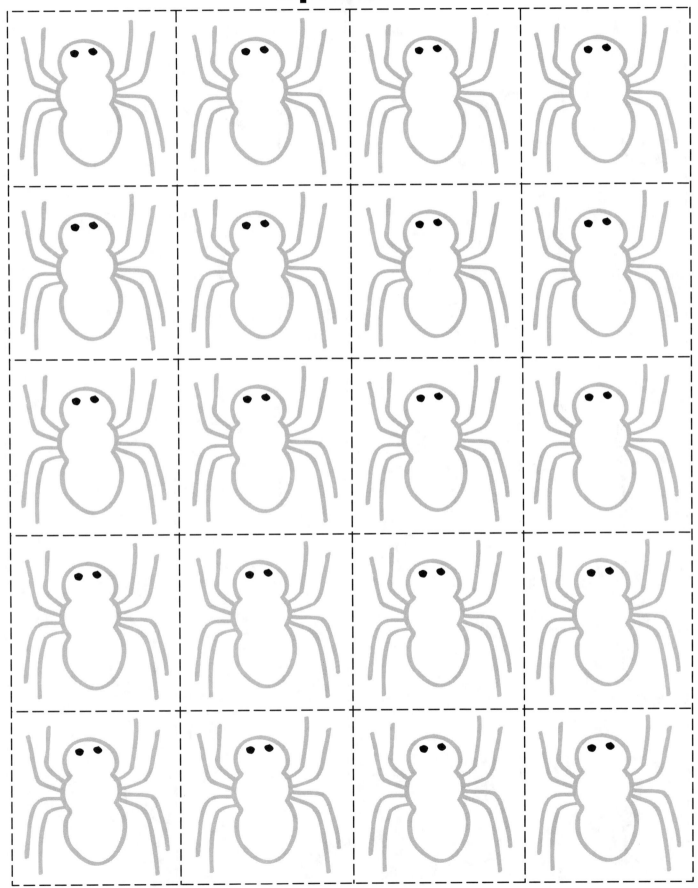

Caterpillars

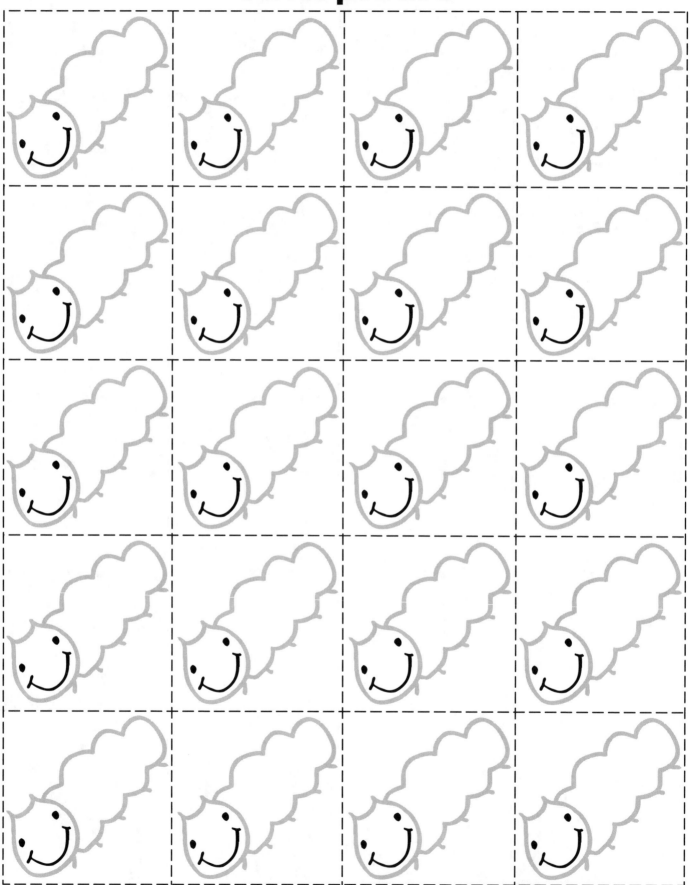

MM2194 • Pattern Projects: Bugs • ©2005 Monday Morning Books, Inc.

Bug Cards
Beetles

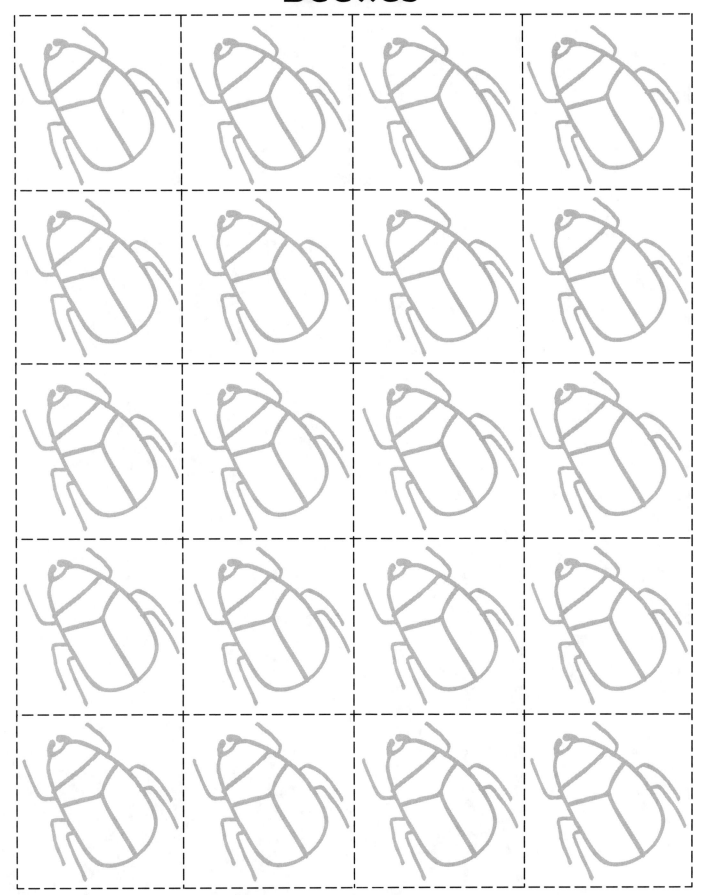

Bug Cards
Fireflies

MM2194 • Pattern Projects: Bugs • ©2005 Monday Morning Books, Inc.

Grasshoppers

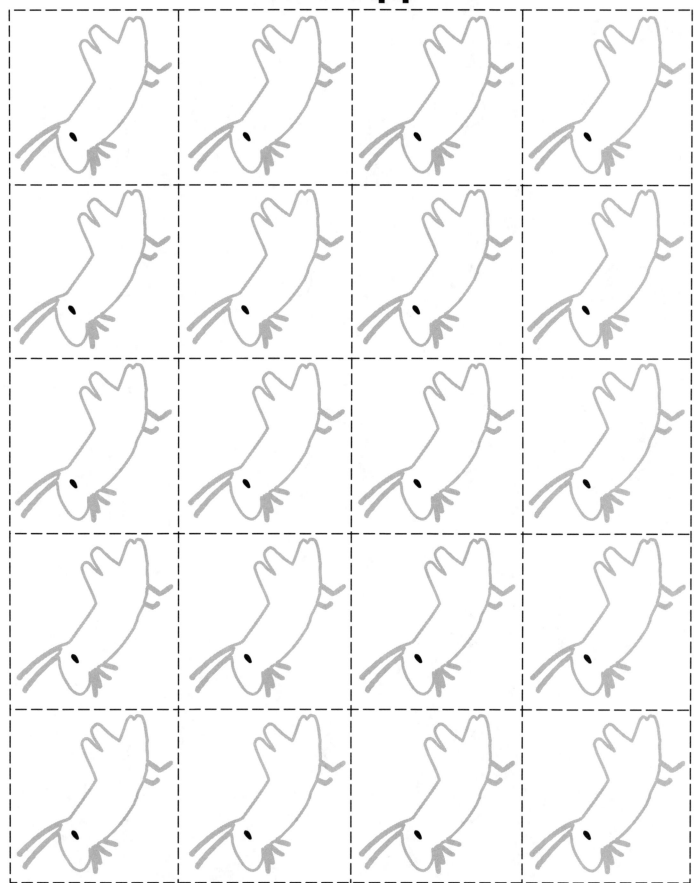

Dragonflies

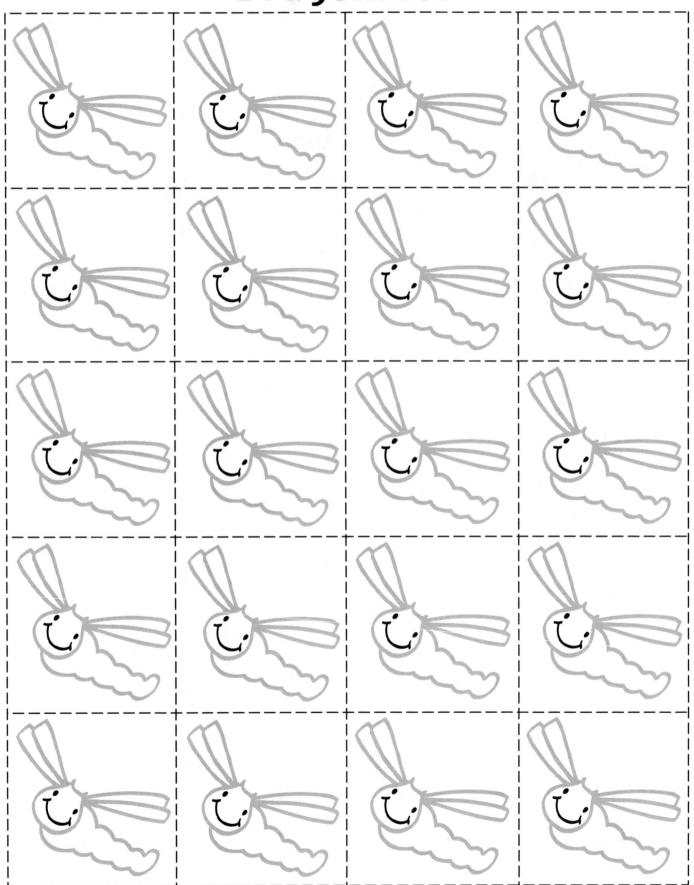

Garden Patterns
Honeycomb

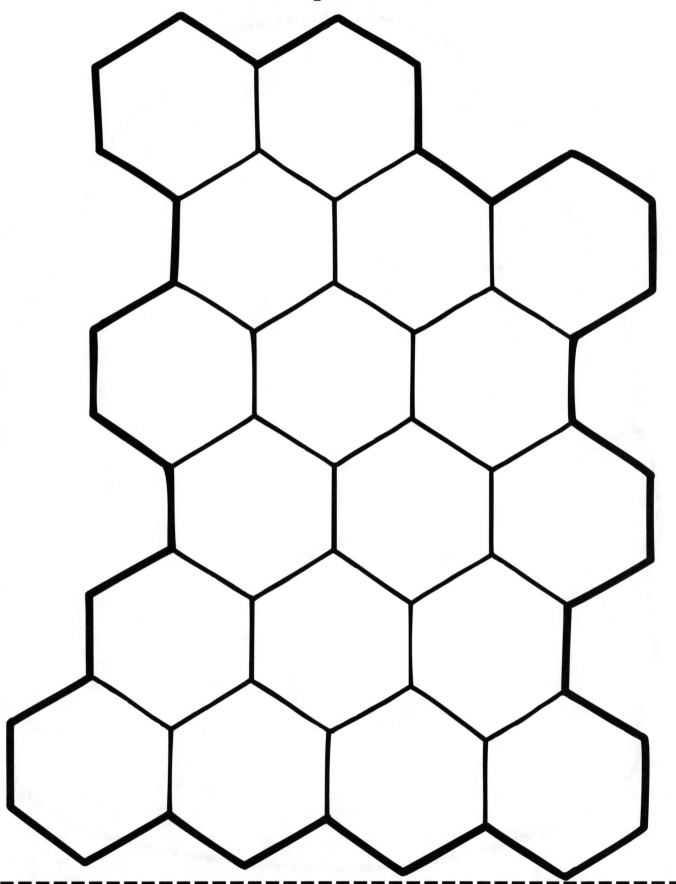

Bee Hive

Garden Patterns
Ant Farm

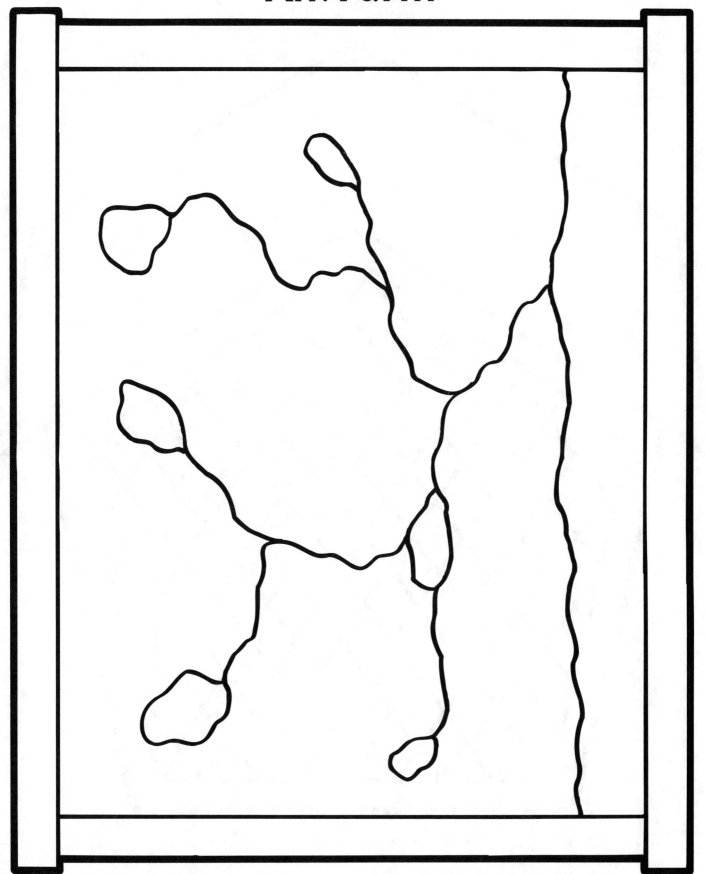

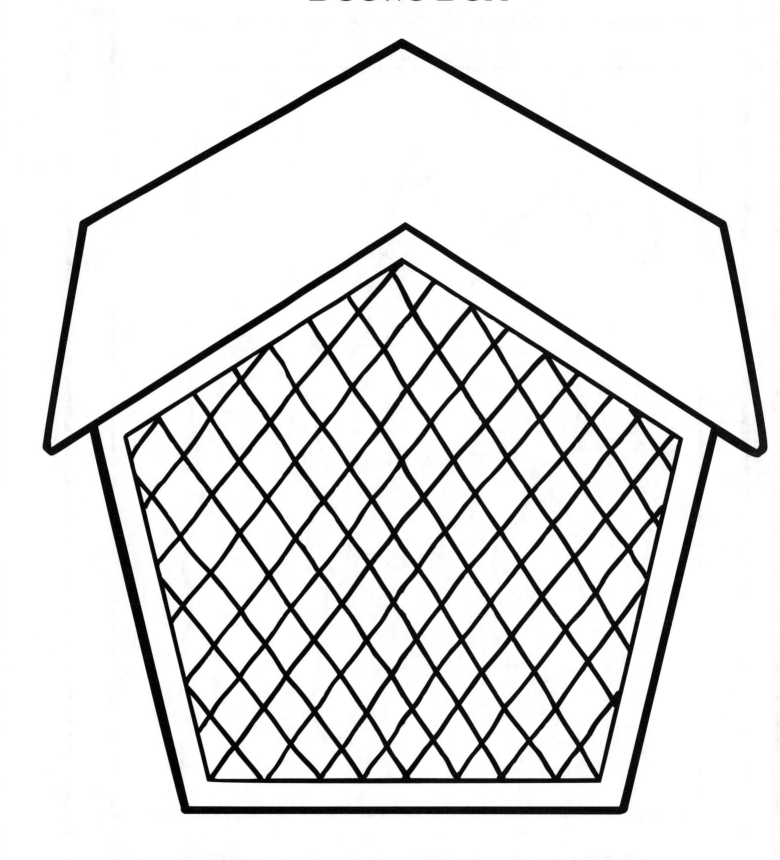

Leaf

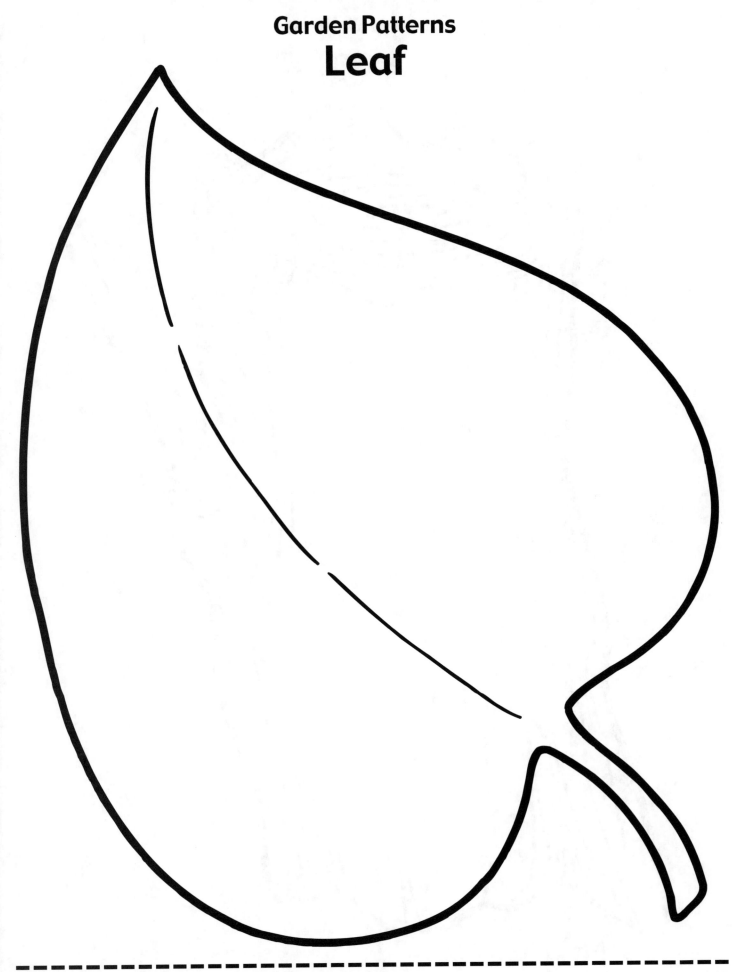

Log

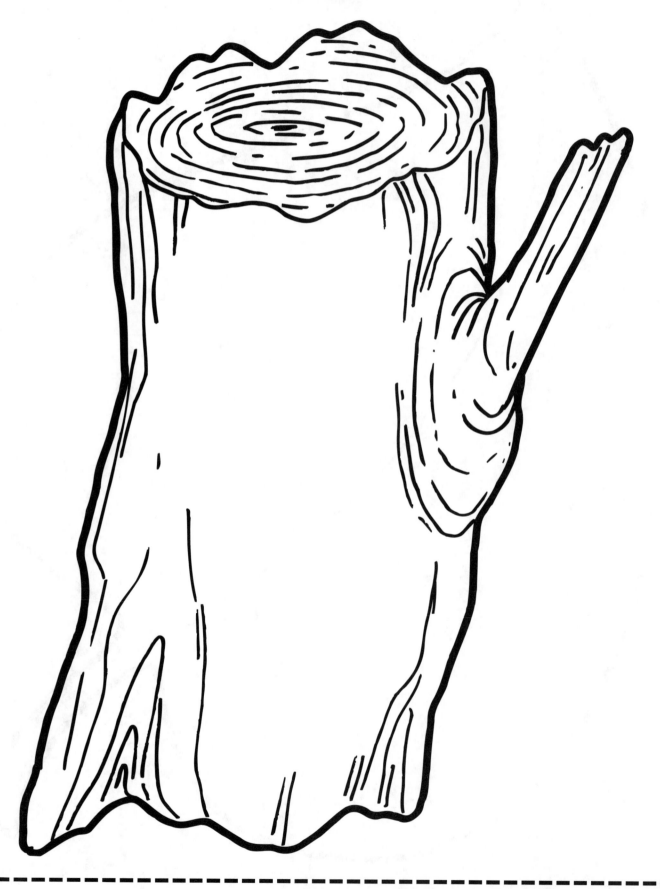

 MM2194 • Pattern Projects: Bugs • ©2005 Monday Morning Books, Inc.

Web

MM2194 • Pattern Projects: Bugs • ©2005 Monday Morning Books, Inc.

Garden Patterns
Net

Bug Button Bookmarks

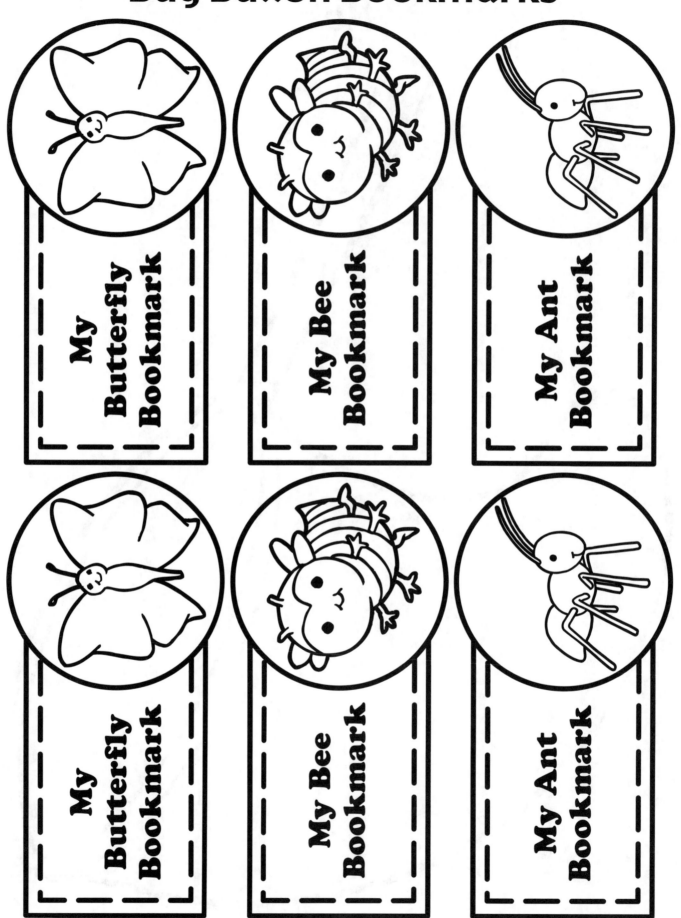

My Butterfly Bookmark

My Bee Bookmark

My Ant Bookmark

My Butterfly Bookmark

My Bee Bookmark

My Ant Bookmark

 MM2194 • Pattern Projects: Bugs • ©2005 Monday Morning Books, Inc.

Bug Button Bookmarks

My
Ladybug
Bookmark

My Spider
Bookmark

My
Caterpillar
Bookmark

My
Ladybug
Bookmark

My Spider
Bookmark

My
Caterpillar
Bookmark

Bug Button Bookmarks

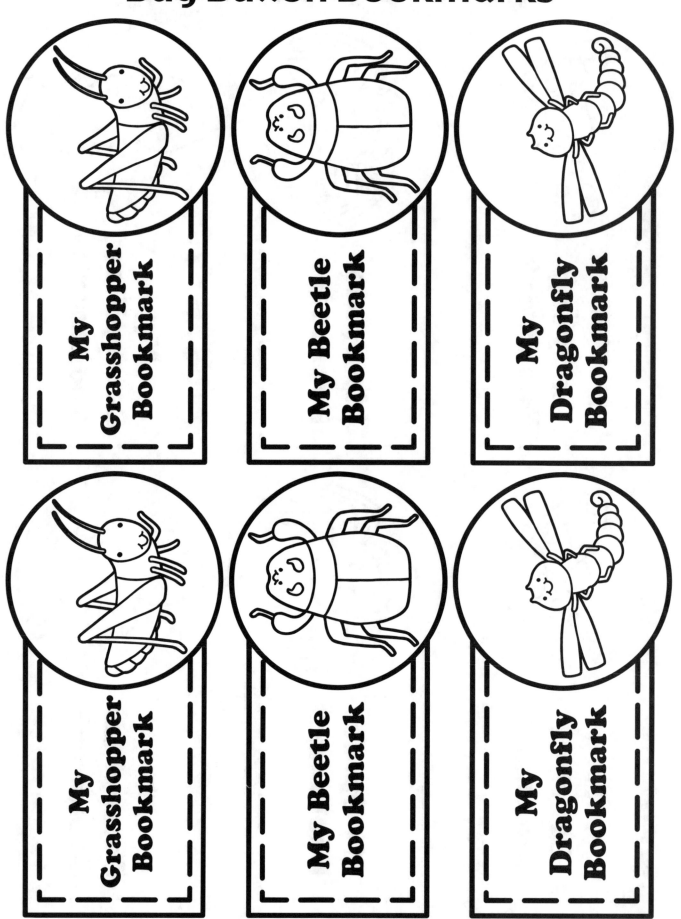

My Grasshopper Bookmark

My Beetle Bookmark

My Dragonfly Bookmark

My Grasshopper Bookmark

My Beetle Bookmark

My Dragonfly Bookmark

 MM2194 • Pattern Projects: Bugs • ©2005 Monday Morning Books, Inc.

Bug Button Bookmarks

Bug Games
Bug Bingo Board

FREE SPACE

Tokens

MM2194 • Pattern Projects: Bugs • ©2005 Monday Morning Books, Inc.

Bug Games
Bug Bingo Board

Tokens

Bug Games
Bugs Match Board

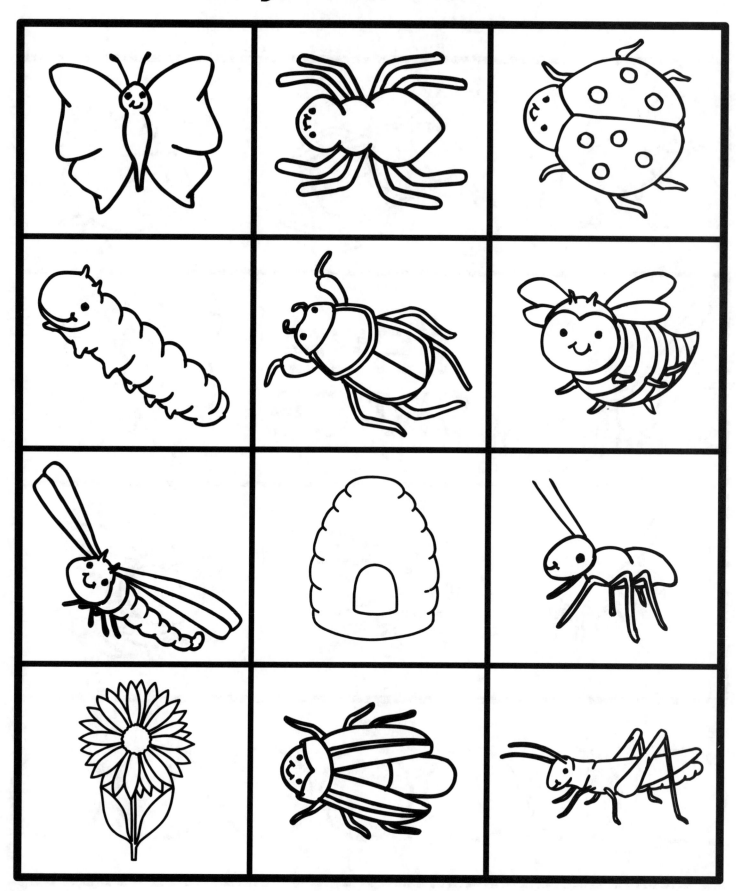

MM2194 • Pattern Projects: Bugs •©2005 Monday Morning Books, Inc.

Bugs Match Board

Bug Games
Bug Cards

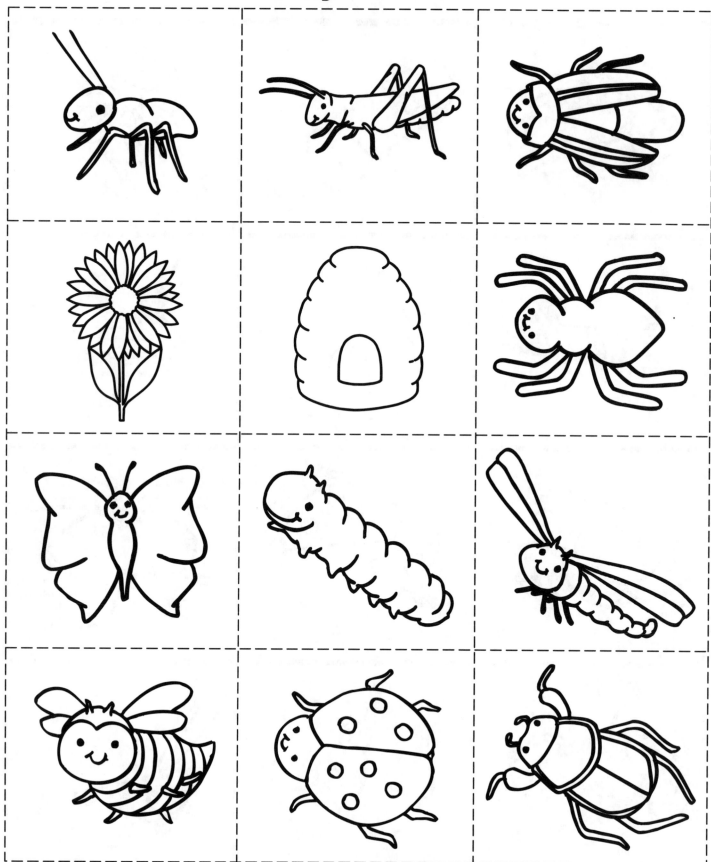

Use these cards for **Bugs Bingo** and **Bugs Match Board** games.

MM2194 • Pattern Projects: Bugs • ©2005 Monday Morning Books, Inc.

Flower Trail

Place spinner or cards here.

Start

Flower Trail Game Board

The End

MM2194 • Pattern Projects: Bugs • ©2005 Monday Morning Books, Inc.

Bug Games
Flower Trail Cards and Spinner

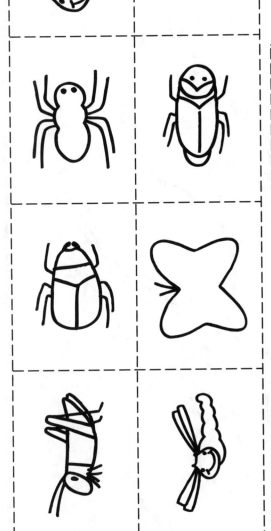

Game can be played with cards or the spinner.

Cards
Reproduce, color, laminate, then cut apart two sets of cards. Provide pawns for two to four players

Spinner
Reproduce, color, cut out, assemble, and place the spinner on the game board.

Bug Bulletin Board Borders

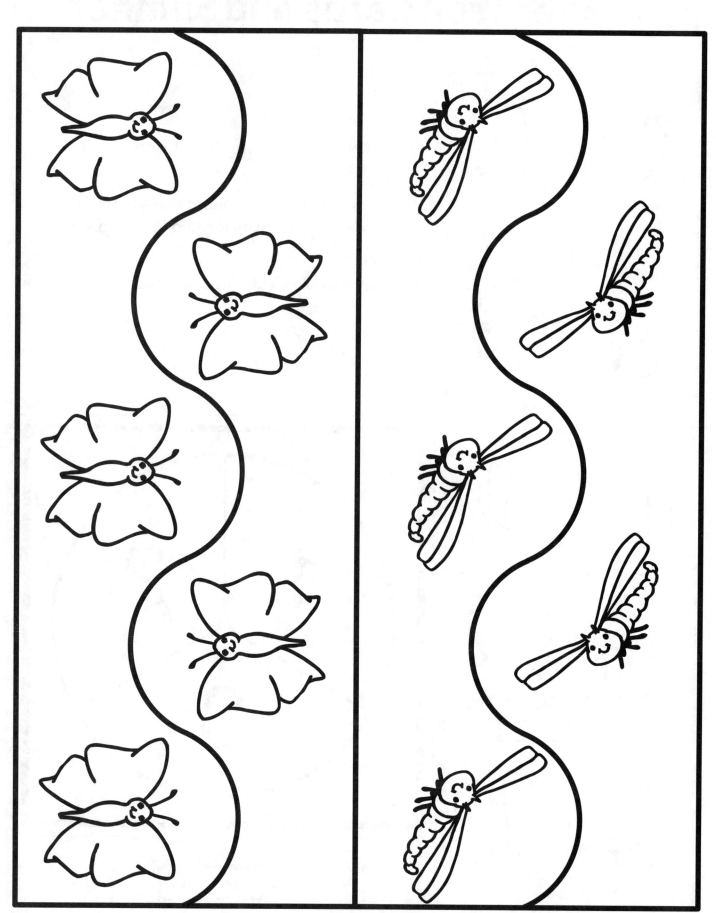

MM2194 • Pattern Projects: Bugs • ©2005 Monday Morning Books, Inc.

Bug Bulletin Board Borders

Bug Bulletin Board Borders

 MM2194 • Pattern Projects: Bugs • ©2005 Monday Morning Books, Inc.

Bug Bulletin Board Borders

Bug Bulletin Board Borders

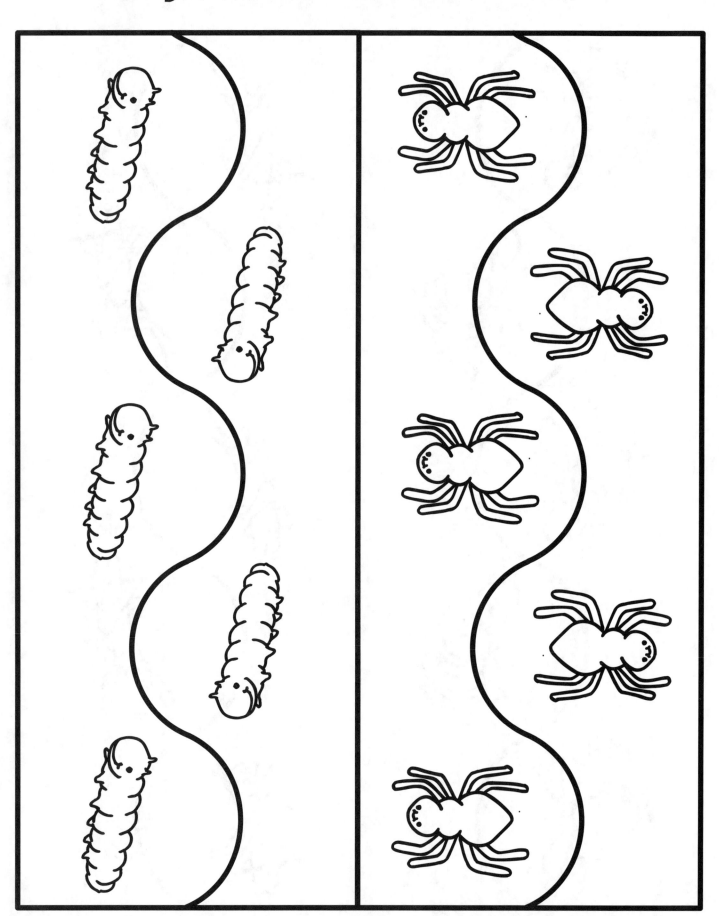

MM2194 • Pattern Projects: Bugs • ©2005 Monday Morning Books, Inc.

Bug Folder Toppers
Butterfly

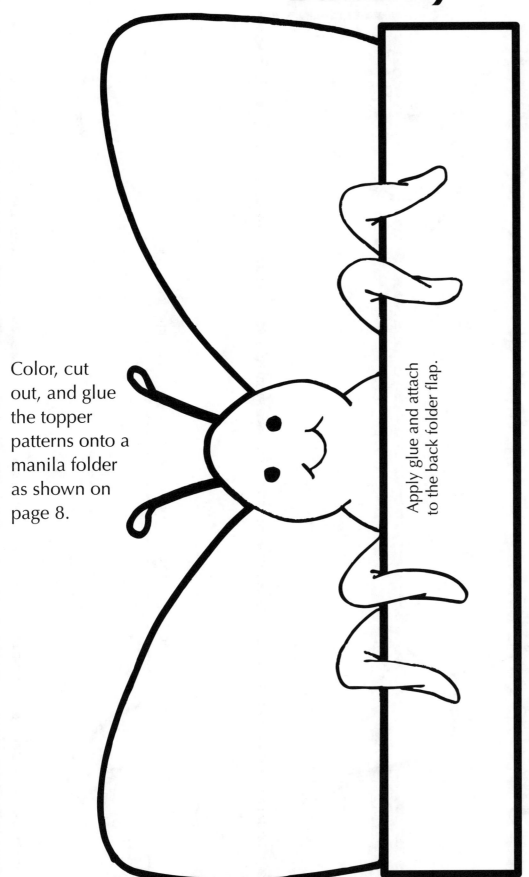

Color, cut out, and glue the topper patterns onto a manila folder as shown on page 8.

Apply glue and attach to the back folder flap.

Apply glue to the back of this pattern and attach to the front folder flap.

Bug Folder Toppers
Bee

Color, cut out, and glue the topper patterns onto a manila folder as shown on page 8.

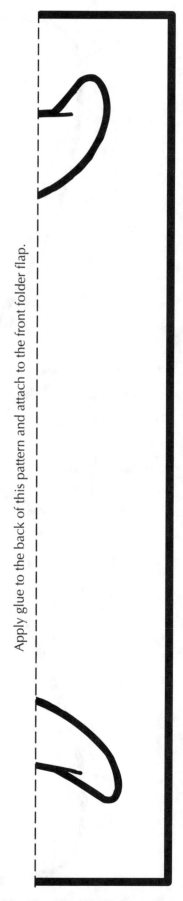

Apply glue and attach to the back folder flap.

Apply glue to the back of this pattern and attach to the front folder flap.

MM2194 • Pattern Projects: Bugs • ©2005 Monday Morning Books, Inc.

Ant

Color, cut out, and glue the topper patterns onto a manila folder as shown on page 8.

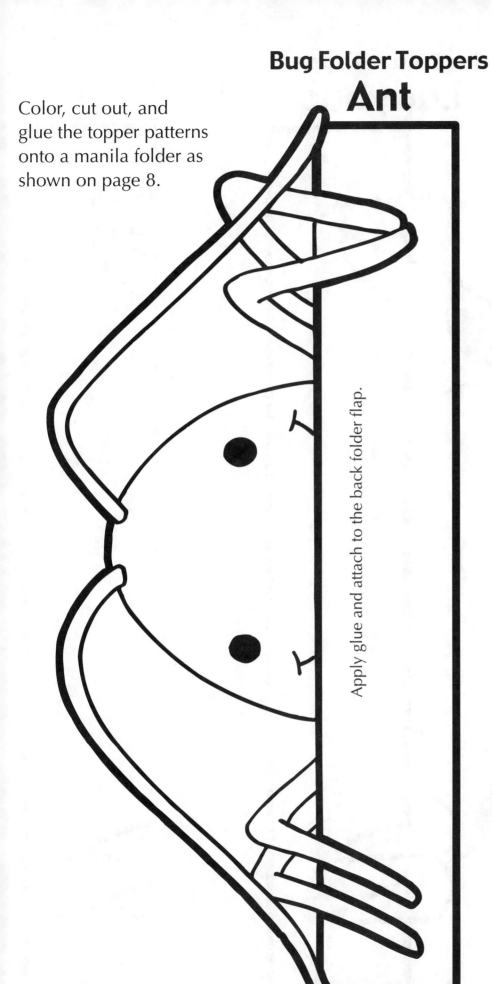

Apply glue and attach to the back folder flap.

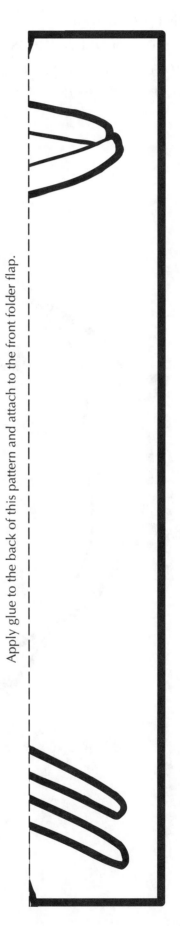

Apply glue to the back of this pattern and attach to the front folder flap.

Bug Folder Toppers
Ladybug

Color, cut out, and glue the topper patterns onto a manila folder as shown on page 8.

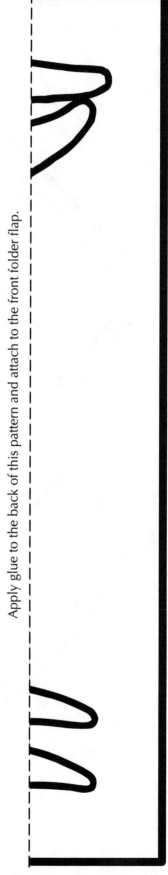

Apply glue and attach to the back folder flap.

Apply glue to the back of this pattern and attach to the front folder flap.

MM2194 • Pattern Projects: Bugs • ©2005 Monday Morning Books, Inc.

Spider

Color, cut out, and glue the topper patterns onto a manila folder as shown on page 8.

Apply glue and attach to the back folder flap.

Apply glue to the back of this pattern and attach to the front folder flap.

Bug Folder Toppers
Caterpillar

Color, cut out, and glue the topper patterns onto a manila folder as shown on page 8.

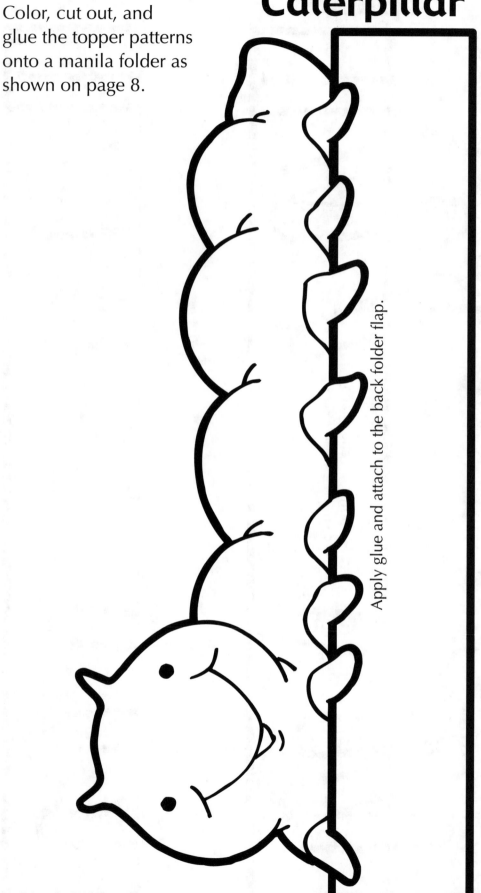

Apply glue and attach to the back folder flap.

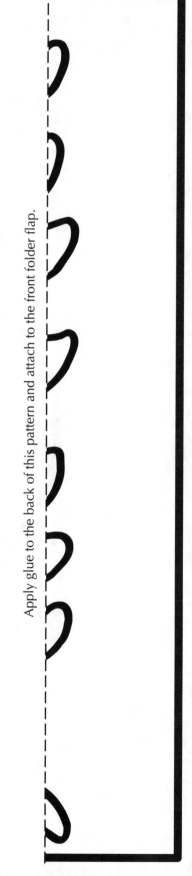

Apply glue to the back of this pattern and attach to the front folder flap.

MM2194 • Pattern Projects: Bugs • ©2005 Monday Morning Books, Inc.

Bug Folder Toppers
Beetle

Color, cut out, and glue the topper patterns onto a manila folder as shown on page 8.

Apply glue and attach to the back folder flap.

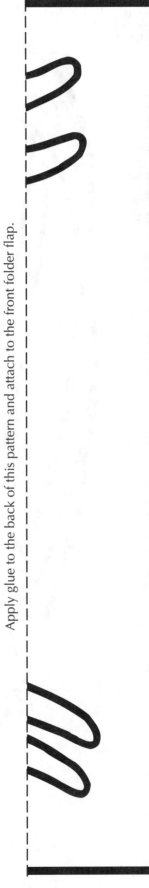

Apply glue to the back of this pattern and attach to the front folder flap.

Color, cut out, and glue the topper patterns onto a manila folder as shown on page 8.

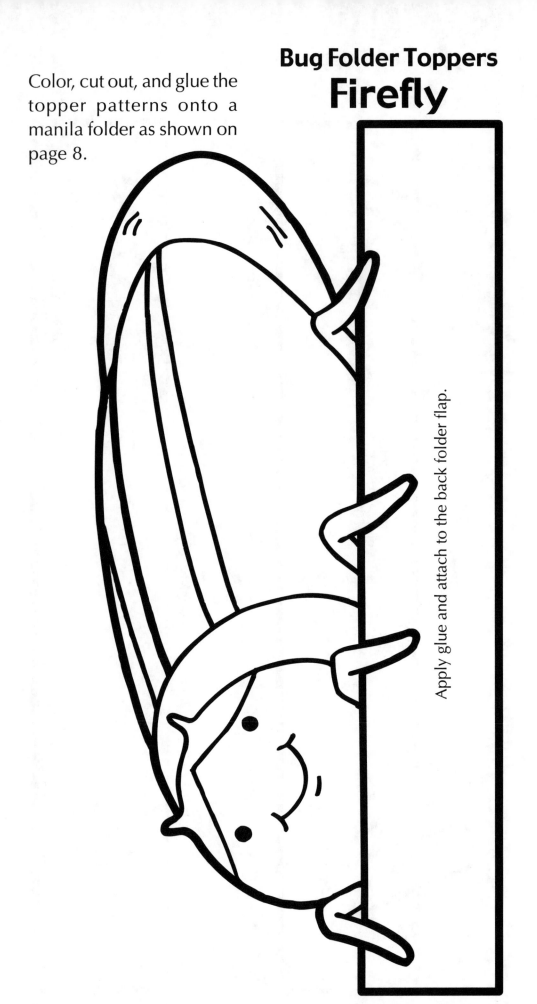

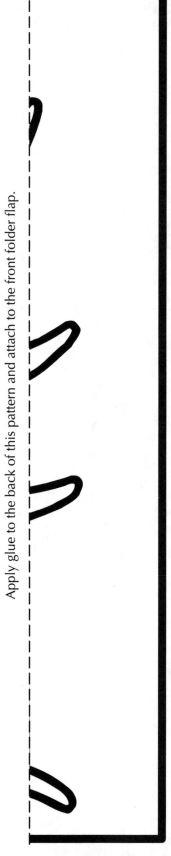

Apply glue and attach to the back folder flap.

Apply glue to the back of this pattern and attach to the front folder flap.

 MM2194 • Pattern Projects: Bugs • ©2005 Monday Morning Books, Inc.

Color, cut out, and glue the topper patterns onto a manila folder as shown on page 8.

Bug Folder Toppers
Grasshopper

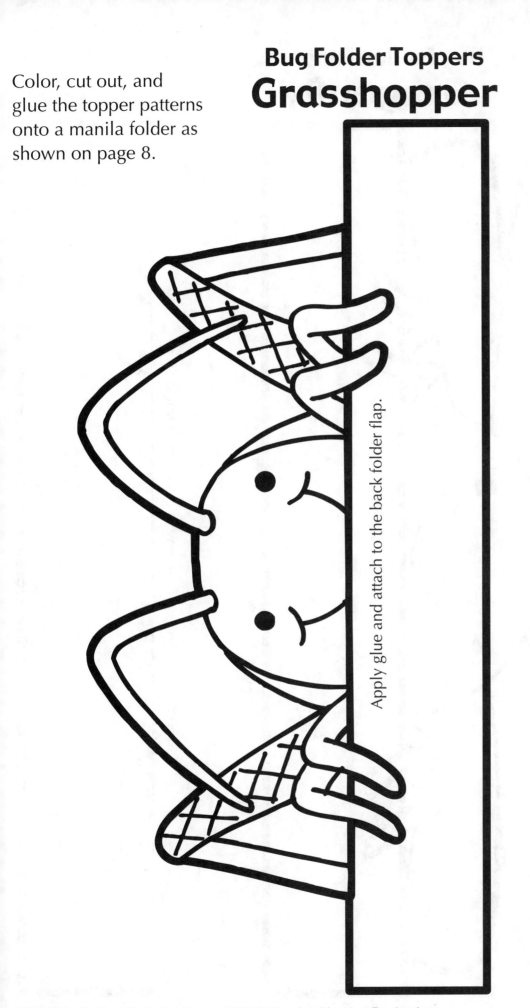

Apply glue and attach to the back folder flap.

Apply glue to the back of this pattern and attach to the front folder flap.

Color, cut out, and glue the topper patterns onto a manila folder as shown on page 8.

Bug Folder Toppers
Dragonfly

Apply glue and attach to the back folder flap.

Apply glue to the back of this pattern and attach to the front folder flap.

MM2194 • Pattern Projects: Bugs • ©2005 Monday Morning Books, Inc.